HOW TO
EVALUATE
INNOVATION
PERFORMANCE
OF
WORKFORCES

Tools and Techniques to
Do It The Right Way

HOW TO
EVALUATE
INNOVATION
PERFORMANCE
OF
WORKFORCES

Tools and Techniques to
Do It the Right Way

DAVID MASUMBA

Thank you to all the healthcare professionals across the globe.

CONTENTS

PREFACE

This book is a framework of tools and techniques for appraising or evaluating innovation performance of workforces in organizations.

It's now common knowledge that in today's innovation-driven global economy, business strategy is about innovation! Innovation! Innovation! And because of the potential for return on investment (ROI) in innovation—in terms of increased revenues, corporate growth and competitiveness, innovation in organizations is no longer a responsibility of a particular functional unit or profession, but a responsibility of everyone from the CEO to the most junior person. According to a number of analysts on innovation, workforce performance trends are shifting away from "routine work" toward innovation performance. What does this shift in work performance mean? It means that for an organization to successfully adopt innovation performance practices, evaluating innovation performance of workforces is an absolute necessity. However, you cannot apply traditional workforce appraisal tools to evaluate workforce innovation performance; you need innovation-oriented tools. This is where the tools in this book come in. For more than ten years, I've been engaged in workforce innovation training and consulting, offered training programs, and interacted with organizational leaders on the topic of workforce innovation. My experience is that most organizations lack tools for evaluating innovation performance of workforces. If organizations want to adopt innovation performance practices across functional units, evaluating innovation performance of workforces is one of the vital requirements. This book offers the tools and techniques of how to do it!

Chapter One

INTRODUCTION

"Twenty years ago the challenge in corporations was quality. *Ten years ago the challenge was* re-engineering. *Today, the challenge is* innovation. *"*

—Gary Hamel

Indeed, there has never been so much emphasis on the role of innovation in fostering sustainable profitability, growth, and competitiveness in businesses like we're witnessing across the globe today. Many studies say that innovation is on the minds of many C-suite executives than never before. For instance:

- In a survey by the Conference Board, a U.S institute that conducts surveys on various topics with CEOs across the globe, about 90 percent of 776 CEO respondents identified innovation as their utmost critical challenge.
- A 2019 study by IdeaScale, a Berkeley, California cloud-based software company, revealed that most organizations look to their employees for new ideas. The study revealed that 72 percent of IdeaScale's customers rely on ideas from their employees.

- In a study by PwC involving 7,757 executives across the globe, 93 percent of executives said that organic growth through innovation will drive a bigger chunk of their revenue growth.

Because innovation is viewed as a fundamental imperative to increasing revenues, along with driving organizational growth and competitiveness by most executives, there's a growing change in the way organizations perceive innovation in terms of whose responsibility it is to innovate and whose responsibility it is to create a climate for innovation across functional units. Many organizational leaders are now embracing the attitude of perceiving innovation as a responsibility of everyone in the organization. However, workforce innovation is not a natural activity, it occurs only if an organization implements necessary practices. So, for workforce innovation to be truly a responsibility of everybody in the organization, specific innovation-oriented systems and practices have to be adopted and implemented. One of the workforce innovation practices critical to sustaining an organization climate where everyone is responsible for driving innovation is assessing innovation performance of workforces on a continual basis. Thus, this chapter focuses on the following aspects:

1. Reason for this book
2. Definition of innovation
3. Meaning of evaluating workforce innovation performance
4. Context and priority areas for evaluating workforce innovation performance
5. Objectives of evaluating workforce innovation performance
6. Structure of this book

1. Reason for this Book

The reason for writing this book is based on the following premises:

Lack of tools for evaluating and rewarding innovation performance of employees
Studies have revealed that the challenge with many companies is how to evaluate and reward innovation performance of workforces. A study by

the *Institute for Corporate Productivity* titled *Innovate or Perish: Building a Culture of Innovation,* revealed that one of the issues that executives are constantly wrestling with is how to assess and reward employees for their innovation performance.

As a way to provide some kind of guidance to companies for rewarding inventor employees, some countries have included frameworks for compensating employee inventors into patent laws. For instance, some European countries (e.g. the UK, The Netherlands, France, Italy, Spain and Hungary) have included employee inventor compensation provisions in their national patent legislations. Other European countries such as Germany, Denmark, Finland, Norway and Poland have enacted specific employee inventor compensation laws.

In my experience as a workforce innovation trainer-consultant, along with data gathered over the course of writing this book, I've discovered that while many organizational leaders emphasize to their workforces to constantly generate innovative ideas, they still subject employees to the traditional performance appraisals and reward models, expecting the traditional performance appraisals to stimulate innovation performance. It is important to know that workforces perform according to the performance evaluation models that they are subjected to and how they are rewarded. There is an old saying that goes, "Behavior that is rewarded gets repeated".

The interpretation is that if the leadership wants to stimulate innovation in workforces, then innovation performance oriented-assessment tools and techniques should be applied. In other words, you cannot evaluate innovation performance of workforces using traditional appraisal methods because traditional appraisals cannot evoke innovation performance in workforces.

Organizations are now seeking to broaden innovation capabilities across functional units

The perception of corporate innovation has changed. The approach to innovation in organizations has been that innovation is the responsibility of

3

specific functional units and professionals. Most organizational leaders have realized that building a sustainable innovation capability is a huge endeavour that should not be left to few specific functional units. So many organizations are now seeking to manage innovation in an integrated way by broadening innovation capabilities across functional units.

A study by Deloitte called *Human Capital Trends* observed that today's innovation leaders are defining innovation broadly to include services, processes, business models, communication, and cost structure improvements across the enterprise. HR can help by aligning people-related factors (such as workforce performance assessment practices) to foster innovation across the organization.

So, how does broadening innovation performance across functional units relate to evaluating innovation performance of workforces? Since evaluating workforce innovation performance generates data about innovation abilities and competencies of employees across functional units, the leadership is able to utilize the generated data to gain insight of how innovation performance abilities are broadening across functional units.

Evaluating workforce innovation performance is an essential element for building innovation capabilities across functional units

Generally, organization capabilities are interpreted as an interconnected set of systems, tools, processes, skills, and knowledge that a company builds over a period of time to drive sustainable growth and competitiveness.

In terms of innovation, one would contextualize innovation capabilities as an interconnected set of systems, tools, processes, skills, and knowledge, which an organization builds to sustain a culture of innovation across functional units.

How does this relate to evaluating innovation performance of workforces? Well, since evaluating innovation performance of employees is critical to advancing corporate-wide innovation performance by evoking and encouraging workforces across functional units to individually—and/or collectively—live up to their full innovation potential, evaluating innovation performance of workforces is a critical part of the interconnected system of innovation-support capabilities essential for creating a climate for innovation.

Traditional management practices have little to contribute to innovation performance

At a conference on innovation held at Harvard Business School, panelists felt that traditional management practices have little to contribute to innovation performance. Many panelists at this conference felt that the current traditional management models are stacked against innovation performance. In the context of traditional employee appraisals, the question is: *Can traditional performance appraisals meaningfully contribute to creating a culture of innovation in organizations?* Certainly not! As stated earlier, in order to effectively systemize innovation across functional units, organizations need to implement different contexts of innovation-support systems and practices, including mechanisms for evaluating innovation performance of workforces.

However, many organizations lack tools for evaluating innovation performance of workforces; this is where this book comes in. As said before, this book offers ready-to-use tools and techniques for assessing and rewarding innovation performance of workforces.

2. Definition of Innovation

In Chapter Two's Step Four, we have given a detailed definition of innovation and why it is important to understand the meaning of innovation when undertaking the process of evaluating innovation performance of workforces. In a nutshell, innovation is a process that involves identifying a problem, then generating an innovative idea—never seen on the market before—and transforming the innovative idea into a solution, then converting the innovative solution into monetary value.

3. Meaning of Evaluating Workforce Innovation Performance

In order to understand what evaluating workforce innovation entails, it is important to understand the meaning of innovation performance. We define innovation performance as: *An expression of innovation skills, abilities, and competencies by executing particular innovation performance-related duties and responsibilities in job positions.*

Thus, evaluating workforce innovation is a systematic and periodic organizational exercise that focuses on assessing or appraising an individual employee's specific type of innovation performance over a particular period. The process includes collecting, analyzing, and recording data about specific innovation abilities and innovation performance of individual employees across functional units.

4. Context and Priority Areas for Evaluating Workforce Innovation Performance

Having defined innovation performance and described what evaluating workforce innovation entails, it is important to understand the context of this book. Context of evaluating workforce innovation is one the first things that should be understood by the leadership of the organization when creating a framework for evaluating workforce or workplace innovation. So, what does the process of evaluating workforce innovation entail? The process entails understanding the types or categories of innovation performance, then zero-in on the priority areas for evaluating workforce innovation. That being said, this book has defined or separated innovation performance into three categories, as follows:

- *Innovative thinking-related performance:* being able to generate specific innovative ideas in the context of the organization's business model and functional activities.
- *Innovation engagement-related performance:* being able to develop and apply techniques for inspiring and instilling innovation performance in the hearts and minds of workforces.

- *Innovation management-related performance:* being able to design and implement innovation-oriented strategies, policies, and procedures.

Chapter Eleven of my book, *Leadership for Innovation*, describes, in detail, what each of the innovation roles entails.

This Book Focuses on Evaluating Innovative Thinking-Related Performance

Innovative thinking-related performance is critical to driving the front end of innovation which is: *identification of problems/needs, opportunities, and the generation of innovative ideas/solutions to deal with the identified challenges and add commercial value to the organization.*

Thus, the model for evaluating workforce innovation performance suggested in this book is focused on innovative thinking-related performance. The other two types of innovation performance—namely, *innovation engagement-related performance* and *innovation management-related performance* are important for creating the mindset and innovation support systems which are responsible for driving the front end of innovation.

Chapter Eleven of the *Leadership for Innovation*, discusses innovative thinking–related roles as duties and responsibilities that are centered on the identification of problems/needs and opportunities, also the generation of innovative ideas/solutions to deal with the identified challenges and add commercial value to the organization. Please note that these duties and responsibilities vary by organization and by functional unit. In functional units, innovative ideas can be generated in either core or support functional units. Some of the core functional units could include the product development unit, manufacturing processes unit, market strategy development unit, and customer service unit. Usually, innovative ideas in core functional units are revenue-based.

Support functional units could include HR, IT, procurement, finance and accounting, corporate affairs, and so forth. Innovative ideas generated in support functional units are mainly centered on cost-saving ideas, and the workforce innovation performance evaluation model should take that into consideration.

The leadership of the organization should ensure that the innovative thinking-related duties and responsibilities in both core and support units are coherently outlined in a simple and clear language in the context of the functional activities of the job position and business model of the organization.

In order to gain from innovative potential of workforces in terms generating meaningful ideas, the context and order of priority areas of innovation performance should be made clear in the job descriptions. For instance, if Company "X" has a job position for an Innovation Strategy Manager, the order of priority areas of innovation performance, in terms of duties and responsibilities, must be coherent and clear. If innovative thinking-related performance is a high priority it must be said so in a clear and simple language. The same would be applied if innovation engagement-related performance or innovation management-related performance is the case.

Furthermore, the job holder (and every employee in the organization) must be made to understand what the organization's policy is on workforce innovation performance, in terms of what type of innovation performance will get rewarded. The leadership should also make it clear that the other types of innovation performance will fall under the traditional reward policy of the organization.

5. Objectives of Evaluating Workforce Innovation Performance

What are the objectives of evaluating innovation performance of workforces? As stated in Chapter One, there are three types or categories of innovation performance roles: innovative thinking-related duties, innovation engagement duties, and innovation management duties. The three types of innovation performance roles have been elaborated in detail in Chapter Three. Bearing in mind the other types of innovation performance roles, the main focus of this book is how to evaluate and reward innovative thinking-related performance of workforces.

That being said, the main objective of evaluating workforce innovation is to encourage, develop, and continually improve the innovation performance of employees (in terms of innovative thinking) and help the organization achieve innovation goals across functional units.

Other objectives include the following:

- Share information about ideation goals
- Communicate the status of innovation ideas
- Understand how employees are faring in each type of innovation performance roles
- Generate data about innovation abilities and competencies of employees across functional units
- Provide a policy framework for rewarding innovation performance
- Generate data that can be utilized in other innovation support strategies
- Provide a one-on-one forum for the leadership to educate their employees about various innovation support strategies, policies, and programs

Details of the above are as follows:

Share information about ideation goals
One of the objectives of workforce innovation performance evaluation is to share information between the employee and the leadership on the desired ideation goals that the employee had set against actual ideation goals achieved during the period under review.

Communicate the status of innovation ideas to employees

Innovation is a process that involves, among other aspects, assessing investable and innovative potential of ideas. Since workforce innovation is exclusively about the involvement of workforces in generation of innovation ideas, it's important that workforces are regularly informed about the status of their innovation ideas undergoing assessment.

So, one of the objectives of evaluating workforce innovation is for the leadership to inform employees of the status of the employees' ideas that are undergoing assessment to determine investable and innovative potential.

Understand how employees are faring in each type of innovation performance roles

This book has separated innovation performance roles or competencies into three categories: innovative thinking, innovation engagement, and innovation management. In most organizations, the focus tends to be on innovative thinking performance roles or competencies. Besides focusing on innovative thinking roles, one of the objectives of evaluating workforce innovation performance is for the leadership to understand how employees are faring in the other two types of innovation performance roles—namely, innovation engagement and innovation management.

Recall that we defined innovation performance as: *an expression of innovation skills, abilities, and competencies by executing particular innovation performance-related duties and responsibilities in job positions.* As stated earlier, this book has defined or separated innovation performance into three categories: innovative thinking-related performance, innovation engagement-related performance, and innovation management-related performance. While the first category of innovation performance is critical to driving the front end of innovation (identification of problems/needs and opportunities and generation of innovative ideas/solutions to deal with the identified challenges and add commercial value to the organization), the other two are important for creating the mindset and innovation support systems which are responsible for driving the front end of innovation.

Provide a policy framework for rewarding innovation performance

Some studies have revealed that many organizations have difficulties in rewarding employee innovation performance. Remember the Institute for Corporate Productivity study mentioned earlier, (*Innovate or Perish: Building a Culture of Innovation*), executives are constantly wrestling with is how to reward employees for their innovative ideas.

So, one of the objectives of evaluating workforce innovation performance is to provide tools and guidelines on how to reward innovation performance of employees across functional units.

Generate data that can be utilized in other innovation support strategies

Remember, the process of evaluating innovation performance generates a great deal of innovation-related data. This data can be utilized in other innovation support strategies, such as innovation talent recruitment strategies, innovation talent succession planning strategies, formulating a corporate innovation strategy, etc. For instance, the data generated could reveal that the organization is lacking in certain innovation competencies and requires urgent action. The leadership can use the data in the process for hiring innovation talent or innovation talent development programs.

Provide a one-on-one forum between the leadership and employees

As stated earlier, creating organization-wide climate for innovation involves great deal of innovation-oriented practices. So, one of the objectives of evaluating innovation performance of workforces is to provide a one-on-one forum between the leadership and employees. Such a forum enables the leadership to highlight, clarify, and educate employees about the various innovation support strategies, policies, procedures, and innovation talent development programs that the organization has enacted or are in the process of adopting.

One-on-one forums also provide an opportunity for the leadership to highlight functional and corporate innovation goals and innovation projects undergoing development.

6. Structure of the Book

This book is structured in fourteen steps in four chapters for designing and implementing a mechanism or framework for evaluating the innovation performance of workforces.

Chapter Two

PREREQUISITES

Overview

There are six steps in this chapter, outlined as follows:

- Step 1: Assessing Current Situation
- Step 2: Describing the Organizational Vision
- Step 3: Outlining the Core and Support Functional Units
- Step 4: Understanding the Meaning of Innovation
- Step 5: Understanding Dimensions of Innovation
- Step 6: Aligning the Meaning of Innovation to Functional Units and Business Segments

The details of the above are as follows:

Step 1: Assessing Current Situation

Assessing current situation is the first step for creating a mechanism for evaluating innovation performance of workforces. The process involves determining whether the organization has included some elements of evaluating innovation performance in the organization's existing workforce appraisal framework.

To understand assessing current situation in the context of evaluating workforce innovation performance, the first step includes: (1) understanding the definition of assessing current situation in the context of evaluating innovation performance of workforces, (2) why it's important to assess current situation, (3) an example of a table for assessing current situation of where the organization stands in relation to the evaluating workplace innovation, and (4) role of the CEO in supporting the exercise.

Definition of Assessing Current Situation

We define assessing current situation in the context of evaluating innovation performance of workforces as: *a process that involves identifying and evaluating various aspects and capabilities of an organization's existing appraisal system to determine the extent to which innovation performance has been included.*

Importance

Assessing current situation provides data that informs the leadership of what innovation performance-related aspects should be included in the framework for evaluating innovation performance of workforces.

Example

Here is an example of a table of assessing current situation when creating a framework for evaluating innovation performance of workforces.

Table 2-1. Assessing Current Situation

Example of a Table for Assessing Current Situation	
Elements of the organization's existing performance appraisal practices: *What are the main and vital aspects of the organization's existing performance appraisal practices?*	**Has the organization included some aspects of innovation performance in the current workforce appraisal system?** If so, outline them
Conducted by:	
Date assessment was conducted:	

CEO Must Support the Exercise

For any major innovation support initiative to succeed, CEO support is critical. Adopting an innovation performance appraisal is a major innovation support undertaking that requires the unwavering support of the CEO and top leadership of the organization. Ensure that the idea of introducing workforce innovation performance appraisal is supported by the top leadership, including the CEO, because without gaining mindshare and support of the CEO, it will be huge uphill exercise.

Some studies have observed that it's almost impossible to systemize innovation across the organization and make it part of the organizational culture without the support of the CEO. For instance, in an interview with *Harvard Business Review Publishing*, when former Chairman and CEO of Procter & Gamble A. G. Lafley was asked about the role of the CEO in advancing and sustaining innovation across the organization, he responded that no innovation thrives in an organization without support of the CEO. In survey of 601 senior executives by Accenture called *"Overcoming Barriers to Innovation"*, one of the key findings was that the role of the CEO in driving innovation performance in an organization was critical.

In short, the role and support of the top leadership in the organization—beginning with the CEO in advancing and sustaining the culture of innovation across the organization—is a key requirement. And since adopting a system for appraising innovation performance of workforces is one of the key aspects of systemizing innovation across functional units, CEO support is vital.

The bottom line is that the CEO should [directly or indirectly] be involved in establishing various committees that will be responsible for overseeing the process of designing and implementing an organization-wide system for evaluating innovation performance of workforces.

Step 2: Describe the Organizational Vision

This section involves describing pertinent aspects of the organizational vision and how they relate to the process of evaluating innovation performance activities.

The aspects include: (1) definition of organization vision, (2) why it's important to understand the organization vision when designing and managing the workforce innovation performance appraisal system, and (3) organizational vision perspectives.

Definition of Organizational Vision

What is an organizational vision? Organizations use different phrases to define their organizational vision. For purposes of this book, a company vision is a picture, expressed in the form of a statement, of what the organization would like to be in a defined time period. The latter part of the definition is what distinguishes a *vision* from a *strategy*—an aspect that is often misunderstood in many organizations.

An organizational vision is normally what the organization would like to be in, for instance, the next three to five years, whereas the strategy is how the company is going to realize that vision.

Perspectives of Organizational Vision

Companies have different perspectives on how to formulate their visions. Some companies have a one-sentence vision statement; others take a multi-dimensional approach in which the organizational vision is expressed from more than one perspective, such as two, three, or four vision perspectives focusing on core concepts. For example, one company's organizational vision might consist of the following four vision perspectives:

- *Market share vision perspective:* Takes into account what the company intends to be like in relation to market share in a defined timeframe.

- *Market leadership vision perspective:* Outlines the company's vision to be a market leader over a specified timeframe.
- *Revenue vision perspective*: Outlines the financial vision of the company over a specified period. In other words, how much revenue does the company intend to generate in the next three to five years?
- *Shareholder value vision perspective*: Outlines the desired percentage of growth in dividends over a specified period.

Bottom line: Whatever style or approach the organization adopts to formulate the organizational vision, it must be simple, clear, and should be understood by everyone in the organization.

Importance

Why is it important to understand the relationship between organizational vision and evaluating innovation performance of workforces? Two reasons:

Align organizational vision with innovation goals

Normally, organizational goals at all levels (i.e. corporate, functional, or individuals) should be aligned with the overall purpose of realizing the organizational vision. Similarly, when it comes to setting innovation goals, individual employees or teams should align their innovation ideation goals with the functional unit innovation goals, and—accordingly—functional unit innovation goals should be aligned with the corporate innovation goals. The corporate innovation goals are derived from the overall vision needs of the organization. The diagram in figure 2-1 provides a simple corporate innovation goal setting flowchart.

Figure 2-1. Corporate Innovation Performance Flowchart

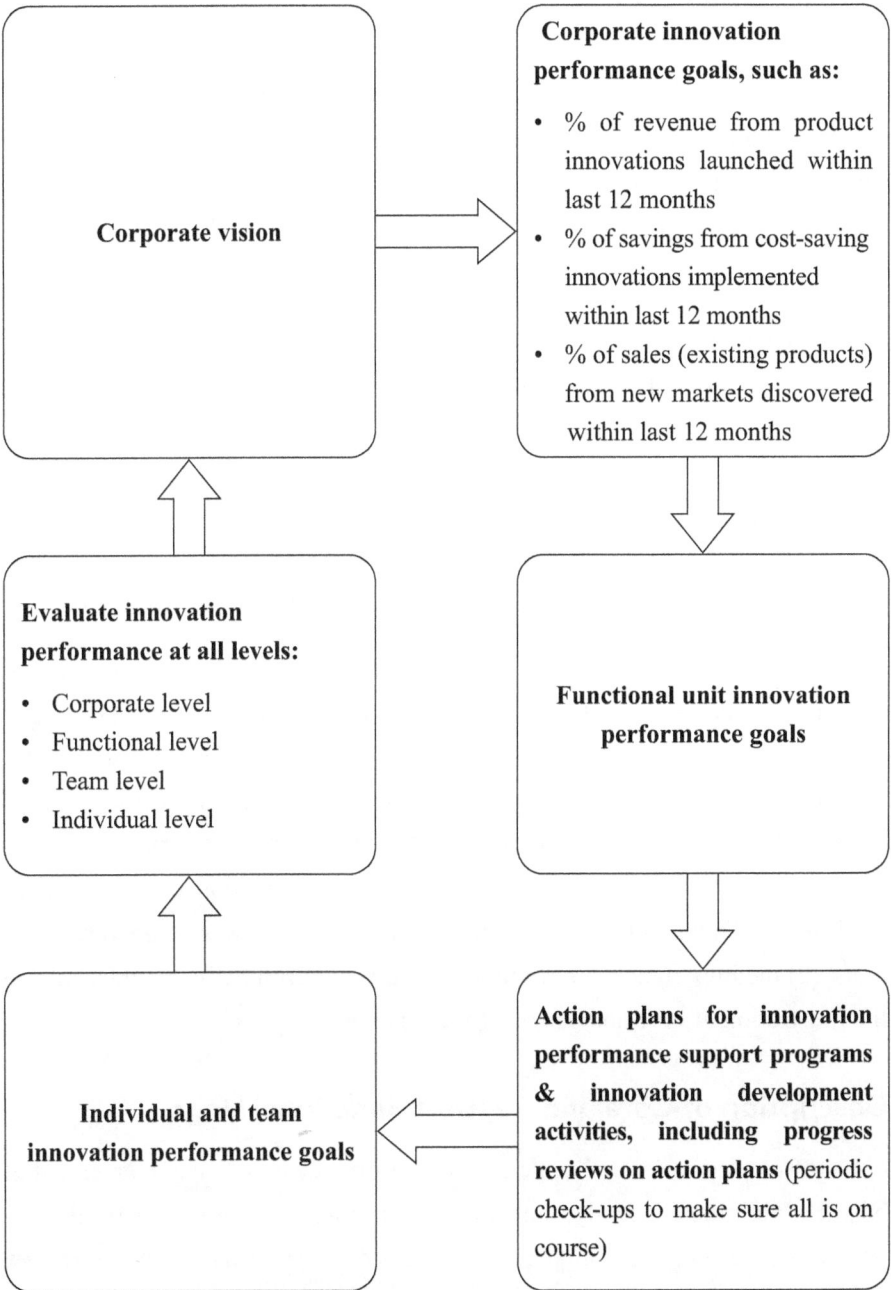

Corporate vision	**Corporate innovation performance goals, such as:** • % of revenue from product innovations launched within last 12 months • % of savings from cost-saving innovations implemented within last 12 months • % of sales (existing products) from new markets discovered within last 12 months
Evaluate innovation performance at all levels: • Corporate level • Functional level • Team level • Individual level	**Functional unit innovation performance goals**
Individual and team innovation performance goals	**Action plans for innovation performance support programs & innovation development activities, including progress reviews on action plans** (periodic check-ups to make sure all is on course)

Adapted from chapter thirteen of the *Leadership for Innovation*

Organizational vision plays a critical role in stimulating workforces to generate innovative ideas

How? Earlier, we defined an organizational vision as what the leadership desires the organization to be like over a specified period. We also mentioned that a vision attracts commitment and energizes workforces in a way that when workforces see that the organization is committed to a vision, it generates enthusiasm about the course the organization intends to follow and increases the commitment of people to work toward achieving that vision. What does this mean?

It means that by creating a clear image of what the organization would become over a specified period of time as a result of innovation performance, it increases the commitment, "buy-in", and enthusiasm of the workforces; it inspires them to not only champion innovation, but to also work hard to contribute to the idea generation pipeline of their functional units.

Step 3: Outlining Core and Support Functional Units

What does outlining core and support functional units entail? Normally, an organization is configured into certain structures, depending on its type of business model and vision. However, in whatever way it is structured, there are two structural categories that every organization consists of: *core* and *support* (back-office) functional units. Thus, this section describes *core* and *support* functions in relation to evaluating the innovation performance of workforces. This includes: (1) the description of core and support functional units, (2) the importance of outlining core and support functional units, and (3) the illustration of core and support functional units.

Description of Core and Support Functional Units

Core functional units are centered on the organization's main or essential business activities. Usually, core functional units are those that are directly involved in driving the organization's mission. For instance, in a furniture manufacturing company, the design and production functional units would be considered *core*, whereas finance and accounting units would be *support* functional units. Also, core units vary from organization to organization, depending on the business model and size.

Support functional units comprise functional activities that are aimed at supporting the achievement of strategic goals and targets of the organization's core business activities. Furthermore, characteristics of functional units vary from organization to organization, depending on the business model and size of the organization.

Importance

Why is it important to outline core and support functional units when designing and implementing the process of evaluating innovation performance of workforces? The introduction to this book mentioned that a culture of innovation in organizations does not occur naturally. It is created by implementing and adopting different kinds of innovation-oriented practices across functional units of the organization.

Evaluating innovation performance of workforces is one of the innovation-oriented practices that can effectively contribute to systemizing innovation capabilities across functional units, thereby contributing to creating a culture of innovation. Since innovation performance of workforces is assessed in the context of the jobholder's current innovation functional roles, it is important that one of the initial steps is to outline the organization's core and support functional units. This exercise should include reviewing and creating innovation performance job descriptions and specifications in all key positions of the organization.

Illustration of Core and Support Functional Units

Let's take the example of Walu Insurance, a fictitious company. Assuming Walu Insurance operates five business units of insurance services:

- Home insurance
- Business insurance

- Auto insurance
- Life insurance
- Health insurance

There are two steps. The first step is to identify product segments in each of the company's five business units.

The second step is to identify the core and support functional units. Let's assume that, besides the five businesses as core units, the company has the following core functional units:

Core units

- Home insurance department
- Business insurance department
- Auto insurance department
- Life insurance department
- Health insurance department
- Marketing department with the following segments:
  - Pricing
  - New markets
  - Product promotion
- Customer service department

Support unit

- Procurement department
- HR department
- Finance and accounting department
- IT department

The third step is to outline the functional units. In this example, two tables are created.

Table 2-2. Business Units and Core Functional Units

An outline of the five business units					Marketing department *(for instance, categories of this functional unit would be…)*	Customer service department *(for instance, categories of customer service would be…)*
Home insurance (state product segments for this category)	**Auto insurance** (state product segments for this category)	**Business insurance** (state product segments for this category)	**Life insurance** (state product segments for this category)	**Health insurance** (state product segments for this category)	• Pricing • New markets • Product promotion	• Before-purchase • During-purchase • After-purchase

Table 2-3. Support Functional Units

Outline functional components that make up each of the support functional units below			
HR	**IT**	**Procurement**	**Finance and Accounting**

Step 4: Understanding the Meaning of Innovation

Lack of understanding of the meaning of innovation can impede workforces from contributing toward driving workforce innovation. So, one of the vital actions that the leadership should take in advancing innovation performance across functional units is ensuring that everyone in the organization is on the same page in terms of understanding the meaning of innovation in the context of the organization's business model .

This section looks at how the meaning of innovation relates to the practice of evaluating innovation performance of workforces. This section includes: (1) the importance of understanding the meaning of innovation when evaluating the innovation performance of workforces, (3) the meaning of innovation, (4) the definition of innovation, and (5) the characteristics of innovative ideas.

Importance

There are two reasons why is it important to understand the meaning of innovation when evaluating innovation performance of workforces:

Workforce innovation performance is a non-starter without understanding the meaning of innovation

The whole process of evaluating the innovation performance of workforces hinges on understanding the meaning of innovation and how the term is translated and actualized into daily performance by workforces in the context of the organization's business model and functional roles across the organization. In other words, without understanding the meaning of innovation in the context of the organization's business model, the process of evaluating workforce performance is a non-starter. So, it is of vital importance to, first and foremost, understand what the term *innovation* entails in the context of the organization's business model and in the context of functional activities across the organization.

Workforces will struggle to perform innovation-related roles without understanding innovation

Workforces will only bring out an innovation-based performance if they understand the meaning of innovation. As similar to the first point, 'innovation performance' is: *an act or process that involves the execution of activities that promote, lead to, or result in an innovation whose ultimate aim is to impact the commercial value aspects of the organization.* However, workforces can only engage in any acts that contribute to advancing innovation if, to start with, they have a clear understanding of what the term 'innovation' means.

Definition

This book defines innovation as a four-part process that involves the following:

Figure 2:2. Definition of Innovation

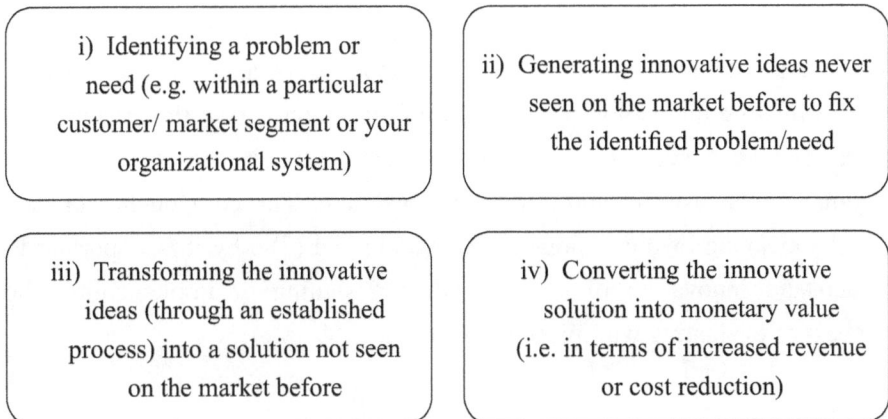

i) Identifying a problem or need (e.g. within a particular customer/ market segment or your organizational system)

ii) Generating innovative ideas never seen on the market before to fix the identified problem/need

iii) Transforming the innovative ideas (through an established process) into a solution not seen on the market before

iv) Converting the innovative solution into monetary value (i.e. in terms of increased revenue or cost reduction)

Chapter Eight of the *Leadership for Innovation* describes how the meaning of innovation is translated into the context of the organization's business model and functional units.

Characteristics of Innovative Ideas

Having described the meaning of innovation, we now look at the characteristics of innovative ideas. Understanding characteristics of innovative ideas is vital and necessary for both the leadership and the workforces because for the most part, workforces will be evaluated on their innovative ideas. So, based on the definition of innovation, characteristics of an innovative idea are:

- New and not seen on the market before
- Aims at meeting customer needs or solving customer problems in a superior manner than before
- Offers benefits to customers in a manner not experienced on the market before
- Contributes monetary value to the organization

Step 5: Understanding Dimensions of Innovation

The fifth component in creating a process for evaluating innovation performance is to understand what the dimensions of innovation entail. Because of the misconceptions that many people have about innovation, it's important that you include in the organization's policy and procedure manual (for evaluating innovation performance of workforces) how the organization interprets the concept of dimensions of innovation in the context of the organization's business model and functional units. This component includes: (1) the meaning of dimensions of innovation and (2) why it is important to understand innovation dimensions when designing or implementing the process of evaluating workplace innovation.

Definition

The term 'dimensions of innovation' means that innovation occurs in different contexts of organizational activities, therefore, dimensions of innovation describes the different ways in which innovation occurs and the degree of change or newness that innovation entails.

In a nutshell, 'dimensions of innovation' is a term that describes two related innovation concepts: *types of innovation* and *innovation degree*. These two concepts are described as follows:

Types of Innovation

Remember, 'dimensions of innovation' is a concept used to describe two aspects of innovation: *where* innovation occurs and *how* innovation occurs. The term 'types of innovation' relates to the context (*where*) in which innovation occurs in the organization's value chain or functional activities. That being said, it is vital to understand that innovation occurs in a variety of functional activities across the organization's value chain. For instance, there are innovation ideas (or innovations) in different contexts of products depending on the nature of an organization's product platforms. There are also process innovation ideas depending on the nature of an organization, marketing innovations, customer service innovations, and a whole host of service innovations. Further details about types of innovation are covered in Chapter Eight of the *Leadership for Innovation*.

Innovation Degree

Dimensions of innovation is a concept used to describe two aspects of innovation: *where* it occurs and *how* it occurs. We have so far talked about types of innovation, which entails *where* it occurs.

This section looks at *how* innovation occurs in any form—or type of innovation, which is referred to as innovation degree (one of the two aspects or concepts of the dimensionality of innovation). The concept of innovation degree is based on the perception that innovative ideas create or add value in varying degrees or extents. Therefore, innovation degree can be defined as the perception of the extent of the newness or novelty of an innovative idea.

Further details about innovation degree are covered in Chapter Eight in *Leadership for Innovation*.

Importance

Why it is important to understand innovation dimensions of innovation when designing and implementing the process of evaluating workplace innovation? Six reasons:

Easy to align evaluation of workforce innovation practices with the organization's business model

Usually, evaluating workforce innovation is based on innovative ideas generated by workforces in the way the organization defines and contextualizes its dimensions of innovation. What this means is that since dimensions of innovation describe the different ways in which innovation occurs, understanding dimensions of innovation helps the leadership of the organization to contextualize evaluation of workplace innovation. In other words, it is easy to align evaluation of workforce innovation practices with the organization's business model and functional activities if the leadership understands the interpretation of dimensions of innovation in the context of the organization's business model and functional activities.

Hard to discharge innovation performance without understanding dimensions of innovation

What this means is that it's difficult for the workforces to effectively discharge innovation performance (through generation of innovative ideas) if they don't understand dimensions of innovation in the context of the organization's business model and their functional activities. It is therefore important for the leadership to ensure that the policy and procedure manual on evaluating workforce innovation outlines, in simple terms, the organization's context of dimensions of innovation.

Motivates workforces to generate diverse innovative ideas

My experience is that many people in organizations misconstrue innovation to mean new products only. While new innovative products are an innovation, they're just one type. In other words, there are different types of innovation—not just about new product ideas. So, understanding the types of innovation encourages and motivates workforces to contribute to the generation of multiple innovative ideas because there are diverse areas that workforces can explore for needs or problems to generate innovative ideas to fix the identified problems, which, in turn, contribute to growth and competitiveness of the organization.

Encourages the ability to set workforce innovation goals

Since generation of innovative ideas occurs within the context of the organization's definition of dimensions of innovation, understanding dimensions of innovation in the context of the organization enables workforces to know how to set individual or team innovation goals in terms of innovative ideas that they desire to generate in the context of the organization's dimensions of innovation. Knowing how to set innovation goals enables everybody across functional units to understand how they are contributing toward advancing innovation in the organization.

Important for formulating innovation performance duties of workforces

Usually, the context of innovation performance duties and responsibilities of workforces across functional units, on which evaluation of workplace innovation is based, is derived from how the organization defines and contextualizes dimensions of innovation. Thus, the importance of understanding the organization's context of dimensions of innovation.

Encourages workforces to track innovation performance

Lastly, understanding the organization's context of dimensions of innovation helps workforces easily track their individual innovation performance because by understanding what dimensions of innovation entail, they are able to know the types of innovation *and* innovation degree they have contributed as individuals. Also, they'll have the keen interest and desire to know (from time to time) the overall innovation performance of the organization at functional unit and corporate levels.

NECESSARY ELEMENTS

Overview

Remember, the Introduction Chapter stated that this book is structured in fourteen steps of how to create a process for evaluating workforce innovation. The steps are divided into four chapters. We have looked at Chapter One so far. Chapter Three looks at Three Steps.

- Step 7: Integrating Innovation Performance Roles in Job Positions
- Step 8: Understanding Factors Driving Innovation in Functional Units
- Step 9: Creating Innovation Goals

Details of the above aspects are as follows:

Step 7: Integrating Innovation Performance Roles in Job Positions

It's important to understand that innovation performance in organizations does not take place in a vacuum; it's enacted or executed by workforces in the form of performance by undertaking specific innovation-related roles. Since evaluating workforce innovation is based on the innovation performance roles or innovation roles undertaken by workforces, it is important for everyone in the organization to understand the organization's context of innovation performance in relation to evaluating workforce innovation. This should be outlined in simple terms in the organization's policy and procedure manual for evaluating innovation performance of workforces.

That being said, this section includes: (1) the definition of innovation roles, (2) aspects for integrating innovation roles, and (3) why it's important to understand innovation roles of each job position when evaluating workforce innovation.

Definition of Innovation Roles

We define innovation performance roles or duties as: *an outline of innovation-related tasks and activities performed by a job holder.*

As stated earlier, innovation roles are separated into three categories: innovative thinking-related roles, innovation engagement-related roles and innovation management-related roles. Chapter Eleven of the *Leadership for Innovation* describes, in detail, what each of the innovation roles entail.

Aspects to Consider

There are three aspects to take into consideration when integrating innovation roles in job positions.

- First, identify areas of innovation priority across business units, segments, and functional activities. Chapter Ten of the *Leadership for Innovation* describes how to outline innovation priority areas.
- Secondly, review current technical duties and responsibilities in all job positions across functional units.
- Thirdly, determine types of innovation roles to be integrated in each job position across functional units. What does this mean?

31

Remember, we said the context of evaluating workforce innovation is one of the first things that should be understood by the leadership of the organization when creating a mechanism for evaluating workforce/workplace innovation. Furthermore, this book has separated innovation performance into three categories: innovative thinking-related performance, innovation engagement-related performance, and innovation management-related performance. In order to maximize innovation performance of workforces, the type of innovation performance that is deemed a high priority in a job position should be stated clearly in the job description. If it is innovative thinking-related performance that is of high priority, it should be stated. This should also apply to innovation engagement-related performance or innovation management-related performance. Chapter Eleven of the *Leadership for Innovation* has described what each type of innovation performance entails, including tables for formulating innovation performance job descriptions and specifications.

Importance

Why is it important to integrate innovation performance duties in job positions for purposes of evaluating workplace innovation? Three reasons:

Provides innovation performance guidelines

Innovation performance does not take place in a vacuum, it's a process that involves an expression of performance by undertaking specific innovation-related duties powered by innovation skills, abilities, and competencies. So, creating innovation performance duties and responsibilities for each job position title guides both employees and leadership on the context of innovation performance and what is expected of the employees in terms of innovation performance.

Creates coherent innovation performance job descriptions

It helps to create a coherent innovation performance job description with clear innovation-performance priority roles in all job positions across functional units of the organization. What does this mean? It means having innovation performance priority roles that are well-written in clear and simple terms, according to the categories of innovation performance, which are: innovative thinking-related roles, innovation engagement-related roles, and innovation management-related roles.

Helps in innovation ideation goal setting by workforces

Since innovation performance descriptions outline the categories and context of innovation performance, it enables workforces to easily identify areas of functional activities for setting innovation ideation goals. It also enables the leadership to easily identify and evaluate different categories of innovation ideation goals set by a team or individual employees.

Helps to identify innovation skill needs

Having innovation performance descriptions enables both the workforce and leadership to easily identify areas of innovation performance duties in which employees may need innovation skill development interventions.

Step 8: Understanding Factors Driving Innovation

Usually, the need for an innovation strategy in companies is mainly influenced by certain internal and external factors. In order to make the process of evaluating workforce innovation effective, (in terms of the process contributing to leveraging innovation to drive organizational growth and competitiveness) it is important to include—in the workforce innovation performance evaluation manual—a component of *how* and *why* an understanding of internal and external factors influencing innovation across functional units is essential when conducting the process of evaluating workforce innovation. This section includes: (1) the definition of internal and external factors, (2) a description of the internal and external factors, and (3) example of a table outlining internal and external factors.

Definition of Internal and External Factors

We define internal and external factors as: *factors obtainable within the organization and business environment that, in one way or another, affect the organization's existence, activities, and future direction, therefore, influencing the innovation decisions of an organization.*

Description of the Internal and External Factors

Chapter Eight of the *Leadership for Innovation* describes numerous examples of internal and external factors that influence organizations to implement strategies for advancing innovation across functional units.

Example:

Here is an example of a simple table for outlining the factors influencing the need for creating a mechanism for evaluating innovation performance of workforces.

Table: 3-1. Outline of Internal and External Factors

Name of department:			
Category of the department's *core* or *support* functional unit:			
Position:			
Date:			
Internal and external factors driving innovation in the functional unit	**Innovation performance roles expected or undertaken by the job holder in light of the internal and external factors driving innovation**		
	Innovative thinking-related roles	Innovation engagement-related roles	Innovation management-related roles
Head of the functional unit:			

Step 9: Creating Innovation Goals

Innovation goal setting is one of the strong attributes of creating a culture of innovation across the organization. Innovation goals contribute to setting the direction and institutional tone about the organization's resolve and desire to be innovation-driven.

Step Nine looks at the relationship between innovation goal-setting and evaluating innovation performance of workforces. This section covers: (1) the definition of innovation goals, (2) the levels of innovation goals, and (3) why it is important to understand innovation goals in relation to evaluating innovation performance of workforces, and (4) how to formulate innovation goals.

Definition of Innovation Goals

Innovation goals are statements expressing the desired future state of innovation performance to be attained within a specified period of time, according to the specified level of the organization (i.e. individual level, departmental level, and corporate level).

Levels of Innovation Goals

Innovation goal setting is the nexus of the whole process of evaluating workforce innovation performance, hence the importance of understanding the levels of innovation goals and how they are connected in delivering value (in terms of creating an innovation-driven organization). The levels and context of innovation goals depend on the nature and size of the organization. The type of innovation goals implies setting innovation goals in terms of the levels of organizational structure. This book has identified four levels of innovation goals: individual level, team level, functional unit level, and corporate level. They're defined as follows:

- *Individual level:* Written statements by individual employees expressing innovation ideas (radical or incremental) that they intend to generate over a specified period of time. Chapter Three's Step Ten of this book has described in detail what workforce innovation ideation goal setting entails.

- *Team level:* Written statements by a team of employees expressing innovation ideas (radical or incremental) that they intend to generate over a specified period of time.
- *Functional unit level:* Written statements expressing the desired future state of innovation performance to be attained within a specified period of time, according to the functional activities of the organization.
- *Corporate level:* Written statements expressing the desired overall future state of innovation performance to be attained within a specified period of time by an organization.

The figure below illustrates the interconnection relationship of the innovation goals.

Figure 3-1. Corporate Vision and Innovation Goals

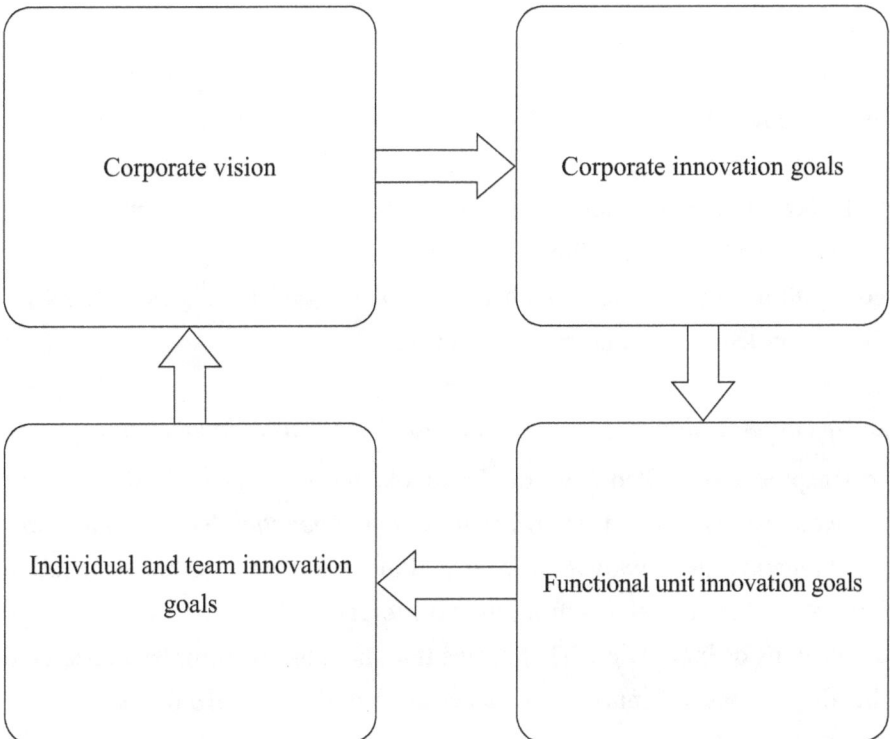

Importance

Why is it important to understand the connection between innovation goals and evaluating workplace innovation? Five reasons:

Helps workforces to have clear innovation performance expectations

As stated before, evaluating workforce innovation performance does not take place in a vacuum, it is a performance appraisal exercise based on predetermined and executed innovation performance expectations. So, innovation goals help workforces determine innovation ideation-related expectations in a specified period of time, and this helps them (workforces) clearly understand what to focus their innovation ideations efforts on.

Stimulates workforces to contribute to innovation aspirations of the organization

Since innovation performance is generally driven by attainment of corporate aspirations, such as revenue goals of the organization, market share goals, customer services goals, etc., innovation goal setting encourages employees to set innovation ideation goals. Once set, workforces will be stimulated to generate innovation ideas to meet their innovation ideation goals, knowing that their innovation ideation goals will potentially contribute toward the achievement of the functional unit and overall corporate innovation goals, ultimately leading to realization of the organization's aspirations for innovation-led growth and competitiveness.

Enhances understanding of organization's dimensions of innovation

In Chapter Two's Step Five of this book, the concept of dimensions of innovation was defined as: *ways in which innovation occurs, i.e. types of innovation and innovation degree.* Innovation goal setting (including innovation ideation goal setting by workforces) is based on the concept of dimensions of innovation. This means that the more workforces understand the dimensions of innovation, according to the organization's business

38

model, the better their capability of generating innovative ideas. In other words, the constant involvement of workforces in innovation goal setting activities helps them understand the organization's context of dimensions of innovation, and this makes it easier for the workforces to generate innovative ideas.

Helps workforces understand the connection between innovation goals and organizational vision

What does this mean? Since individual employees create their innovation goals based on, mostly, contributing toward meeting higher organizational innovation goals (such as functional unit or corporate level innovation goals), workforce innovation ideation goal setting helps workforces to understand the context of all levels of innovation goals and how they are connected to the overall vision of the organization. What this means is that when workforces understand how to phrase workforce innovation ideation goals, it helps them understand the different levels of innovation goals, such as functional unit and corporate innovation goals—also how each of the three levels of innovation goals (individual , functional unit, and corporate) are connected to realizing the overall vision of the organization. This encourages workforces to make innovation ideation habitual and contributes, in a big way, to making the organization innovation-driven.

Makes it easy to track innovation performance of workforces

Innovation goal setting makes it easy for both workforces and leaders to determine and track innovation ideation practices of employees; and makes it easy to determine to what extent they are delivering on their innovation ideation promises and expectations.

How to Formulate Innovation Goals

There are a number of aspects to consider when formulating the different levels of innovation goals, i.e. workforce innovation ideation goals (individual/team levels), functional unit innovation goals, and corporate innovation goals. Chapter Three of this book has a section (Step Ten) about how to formulate workforce ideation goals. For the other types of innovation goals (function unit and corporate levels), chapter thirteen of the *Leadership for Innovation* provide detailed descriptions of aspects to take into consideration when formulating functional unit and corporate innovation goals.

Chapter Four

EVALUATION TOOLS AND REWARD MODEL

Overview

In Chapter One of this book, we described some reasons why evaluating workforce innovation is a vital practice—some of the reasons are: (1) Lack of tools for evaluating and rewarding innovation performance of employees. (2) Organizations are now seeking to broaden innovation capabilities across functional units. (3) Evaluating innovation performance of workforces is an essential element for building innovation capabilities cross-functional. (4) Traditional management practices have little to contribute to innovation.

The purpose of this book is to provide a framework that contributes to creating and sustaining a culture of innovation in organizations. That being said, the book has already detailed nine steps that are divided into three chapters. Chapter Four completes the steps of creating a framework for evaluating innovation performance of workforces. This chapter contains the following steps:

- Step 10: Workforce Innovation Ideation Goals
- Step 11: Innovation Idea Submission

- Step 12: Employee Innovation Ideation Review
- Step 13: Idea Assessment Progression
- Step 14: Workforce Innovation Reward Model

Step 10: Workforce Innovation Ideation Goals

Please recall, Step Nine described what functional unit and corporate innovation goals are, their importance, and how to formulate them. It's important to understand that achievement of functional unit and corporate innovation goals does not emanate from the blues, it involves contribution from workforces in terms of the generation of various types and degree of innovative ideas. In other words, workforce innovation goals feed into higher level (functional unit and corporate) innovation goals. Therefore, this section focuses on workforce innovation ideation goals. This section covers: (1) the definition of workforce innovation ideation goals, (2) the importance of workforce innovation ideation goals, (3) characteristics of workforce innovation ideation goals, and (4) creating workforce innovation ideation goals.

Definition

As earlier stated, we define workforce innovation ideation goals as: *written statements by individual employees or team members expressing innovation ideas (radical or incremental) that they intend to generate over a specified period of time.*

Importance

Why is workforce innovation ideation goal setting important? Five reasons:

Organizations' innovation aspirations depend on employee innovation ideation

In the introduction, we stated that studies show innovation as a top priority to many corporate leaders across industries for purposes sustaining of growth

42

and competitiveness. In order to realize the aspirations of innovation-led growth and competitiveness, many organizations are developing innovation support systems, such as involving every employee in driving innovation. However, realization of organizations' innovation aspirations largely depend on the employees' innovation ideation aspirations and the employees' ability to actualize those aspirations.

Workforce innovation ideation goals feed into the mainstream innovation goals of the organization

Remember, in Step Nine, we talked about the levels of innovation goals being individual/team level, functional unit, and corporate level? What this means is that workforce innovation ideation goal setting forms a crucial component of the means-and-ends chain relationship that exists within the innovation goals hierarchy of an organization. With that, low-level innovation goals (workforce innovation ideation goals) lead to the accomplishment of high-level innovation goals (functional unit and corporate innovation goals). Because of the role that workforce innovation ideation goals play in realizing overall innovation performance of an organization, the leadership should ensure that workforces across functional units have the ability to create and execute innovation ideation goals in the context of the workforces' functional activities.

Helps workforces to direct their ideation efforts

A number of studies on goal setting, including studies by Dr. Edward Locke (an expert on the theory of goal setting), have long revealed that goal setting helps one to know what they're desiring to achieve. In the context of idea generation, the ability by workforces to set innovation ideation goals helps individual employees to determine how to direct their innovation generation efforts in terms of what type and degree of innovative ideas to focus on in their functional roles based on their innovation ideation goals.

Workforces will understand their overall contribution to innovation

Since workforce innovation ideation feeds into the functional and corporate innovation goals of the organization, innovation ideation goal setting enables workforces to determine their contribution toward advancing innovation in their functional units and to the organization as a whole.

Characteristics of Workforce Innovation Ideation Goals

It's important to understand that creating innovation ideation goals is one thing; creating innovation ideation goals that effectively contribute to the overall achievement of the organization's aspirations of innovation-led growth and competitiveness is another. The latter is a crucial aspect. The question is: what are the characteristics of good workforce innovation ideation goals? Here are the five characteristics:

- Workforce innovation ideation goals should aim to generate innovative ideas that are focused and specifically targeted at characteristics of the identified need, problem, or business opportunity.
- Specify the type of innovation on which to focus the innovation idea, i.e. indicate whether the innovation idea generation goal is to focus on product innovative ideas, the service innovative ideas process, marketing innovative ideas, customer service innovative ideas, etc.
- Specify the innovation degree which ideation efforts will focus on, i.e. whether it's radical or incremental innovative ideas that one intends to focus on.
- Innovation ideation goal should comprise both descriptive and quantitative characteristics. For example, "Generate three incremental procurement innovation ideas by May 30, 2020 with each idea, not requiring more than "X" financial resources to develop, aimed at fixing procurement process problem "Y".
- Specify the time period over which one intends to generate the innovation ideas. For example, by date "X".

Innovation ideation goal equation

The above characteristics could be summarized as: (innovation challenge) + (type of innovation idea) + (innovation degree) + (time frame) = innovation ideation goal

Illustration: Creating Workforce Innovation Ideation Goals

Let's return to our fictitious company Walu Insurance, which has five business units of insurance services. Assume we wish to create a worksheet that for workforces would be using to set their innovation ideation goals.

The first step is to identify business units which are core units. The second step is to identify support functional units as follows:

Core units
- Business units
    - Home insurance department
    - Auto insurance department
    - Business insurance department
    - Life insurance department
    - Health insurance department
- Marketing department
    - Pricing
    - New markets
    - Product promotion
- Customer service department

Support units
- Procurement department
- HR department
- Finance & Accounting department
- IT department

Third step is to create a worksheet for formulating workforce innovation ideation goals. Below is an example of the worksheet.

Table 4-1. Formulating Workforce Innovation Ideation Goals

Name of staff: _____ Position: _____			
Department: _____ Date: _____			
Type of Innovation: State by use of a tick against the business unit or functional category to focus innovation ideation:	**Timeframe:** The period over which one intends to generate the innovative ideas	**Innovation degree:** The extent of innovation newness that one intends to focus their innovation ideation on, i.e. *radical* or *incremental* innovative ideas	**Innovation challenge questions:** Challenge questions that one has identified to focus their innovation ideation on
Business unit innovative ideas • Home insurance innovative ideas • Business insurance innovative ideas • Auto insurance innovative ideas • Life insurance innovative ideas • Health insurance innovative ideas			
Marketing innovative ideas • Pricing • New markets • Product promotion			

table continues on next page

Type of Innovation: State by use of a tick against the business unit or functional category to focus innovation ideation:	Timeframe: The period over which one intends to generate the innovative ideas	Innovation degree: The extent of innovation newness that one intends to focus their innovation ideation on, i.e. *radical* or *incremental* innovative ideas	Innovation challenge questions: Challenge questions that one has identified to focus their innovation ideation on
Customer service innovative ideas • Before purchase innovative ideas • During purchase innovative ideas • After purchase innovative ideas			

Example: Workforces should state, in sentence form, the innovation ideation goals. For instance:

1. "Generate two incremental customer service innovation ideas by May 30, 2020 with each idea, not requiring more than "X" financial resources to develop, aimed at fixing customer service problem "Y".

2. _____

3. _____

	For radical innovative ideas	For incremental innovative ideas
Number of innovation ideation goals set		

Table 4-2. Formulating Workforce Innovation Ideation Goals in Support Functional Units

| Name of staff: _____ Position: _____ |
| Department: _____ Date: _____ |

Type of innovation: Remember, innovation in support units is aimed at cost saving or efficiency; so, state by use of a tick against the functional unit to focus innovation ideation:	Timeframe: The period over which one intends to generate the innovative ideas	Innovation degree: The extent of innovation newness that one intends to focus their innovation ideation on, i.e. *radical* or *incremental* innovative ideas	Innovation challenge questions: Challenge questions that one has identified to focus their innovation ideation on
Cost saving innovative ideas • Procurement unit • HR unit • IT unit • Finance and Accounting unit			

Number of innovation ideation goals set	For radical innovative ideas	For incremental innovative ideas

Step 11: Innovation Idea Submission

It is often said that organizations do not lack ideas, but effective systems to encourage generation of ideas from workforces and the capturing of the right ideas for further development.

Once employees have set their innovation ideation goals, the next step is generation of innovation ideas to fulfill the various radical or incremental innovation ideation goals they've set. Once employees generate their ideas, the next question is in where they should submit their ideas. So, this section focuses on creating a tool for employees to submit their innovation ideas. We've referred to this process as *innovation idea submission*.

This section covers: (1) the definition of innovation idea submission, (2) the importance of innovation idea submission, and (3) an example of an innovation idea submission worksheet.

Definition

Innovation idea submission is defined as: *a resource for employees to write down ideas that they perceive innovative, then submit them for consideration to a supervisor, manager, or an idea assessment committee to determine whether or not the idea has investable innovation potential.*

In a nutshell, the idea submission stage kickstarts the process of considering innovative and investable potential of an idea.

Importance

Why is the innovation idea submission process important? Two reasons:

Encourages workforces to generate ideas
The whole concept of innovation hinges on generation of innovative ideas. What this entails is that with the existence of the innovation idea submission

process as a tool to guide workforces to whom in the organization they should refer their innovation ideas, it plays a significant role in encouraging workforces to generate ideas because to start with workforces, know that there is a process that will attend to their ideas.

An effective process for capturing innovative ideas from workforce is vital

Innovative ideas serve as the main and basic resource for a company to realize it's aspiration of being innovation-driven. However, there are many moving parts for an organization to achieve and sustain innovation-led growth and competitiveness, including having an effective process for capturing innovative ideas from workforces. A number of studies and reports on most innovative companies suggest that having a system for capturing innovation ideas from workforces is one of the main aspects to implement if an organization is to succeed in making innovation every employee's responsibility across functional units.

Example

Below is an example of the innovation idea submission form.

Table 4-3. Innovation Idea Submission

Name of employee(s): _____ Position: _____	
Department: _____	
Date of submitting the innovation idea: _____	

Type of innovative idea? **For instance, is it:**	**Describe the innovative idea.** **What is it?**
• Home insurance innovative idea • Business insurance innovative idea • Auto insurance innovative idea • Life insurance innovative idea • Health insurance innovative idea • Marketing innovative idea • Customer service innovative idea **Cost saving innovative ideas** • Procurement unit • HR unit • IT unit • Finance and Accounting unit	
What need or problem does the innovative idea seek to solve?	What innovation degree is the idea? Is it *radical* or *incremental*

table continues on next page

Type of innovative idea? For instance, is it:	Describe the innovative idea. What is it?
How will the innovative idea solve the need or problem?	What benefits will the innovation idea contribute to the organization, clients, and community?
Comments and decision by relevant assessment committees on whether the idea should: • *Proceed for further assessment* • *Be rejected* • *Be put on hold*	
Name of committee responsible for assessing the idea:	
Names and positions of committee members:	

Step 12: Employee Innovation Ideation Review

Earlier when describing idea generation goals, we said that like seeds that require good conditions to germinate, generation of innovative ideas by workforces requires the presence of organizational conditions that support innovation. There are various innovation support initiatives that organizations enact to create organizational conditions that can stimulate and drive innovation performance across functional units. Such initiatives include tools to help workforces with the innovation ideation process. So far, this book has suggested some tools that can help and encourage workforces generate innovation ideas. This section looks at another tool that can contribute to encouraging workforce idea generation across functional units. The tool is called "employee innovation ideation review". This section covers: (1) the definition of employee innovation ideation review, (2) the importance of adopting the employee innovation ideation reviews, and (3) an example of the employee innovation ideation review table.

Definition

"Employee innovation ideation review" is defined as: *a periodic meeting between employees and their superiors to determine the following:*

- Whether the employees set innovation ideation goals over a particular period; if they did, what type of goals are they?
- Whether the employees have, over a particular period, generated and submitted any innovation ideas.
- Whether the submitted innovation ideas have been subjected to the organization innovation development process.

Importance

There are many reasons why an employee innovation ideation review is important. Four reasons:

Motivates workforces to generate innovative ideas
The basic and overall purpose of evaluating innovation performance of workforces is to contribute toward advancing innovation across the organization by providing a tool aimed at inciting generation of innovative ideas from workforces. So, by regularly checking the innovation ideation goals of the workforces, it encourages and motivates them to generate innovation ideas since employees would want to show that they are part and parcel of the innovation performance mission of the organization.

Encourages workforces to generate real innovative ideas

By holding regular innovation ideation review meetings with workforces, it's an indication of the leadership's appreciation and support for employees efforts to contribute to advancing innovation in the organization. And this encourages workforces to work hard and generate innovative ideas with high potential for success, knowing that their organization is committed to seeing employees succeed in contributing to the innovation ideation pipeline of the organization.

It's an opportunity to inspire workforces to keep generating innovative ideas

One of the critical factors that contributes to sustaining innovation performance as an ongoing process across functional units of an organization is if (among other aspects) the majority of workforces develop passion and emotional interest in being a part of driving innovation across the organization. It is said that people have a built-in need to believe in something when they are convinced that there is something in it for them. Once they establish that there is something for them, they will own it and they will invest incredible amounts of energy and dedication to bring about its fruition.

Innovation ideation review meetings provide a great opportunity for leaders to articulate, inspire, and educate employees about *why* and *how* innovation is a critical ingredient for increasing profitability, enhancing competitiveness and growth to the organization, and how innovation ideation enhances career development and financial benefits to workforces, thus the need for employees to be passionate about innovation ideation habits.

Provides opportunity to discuss strengths and weaknesses of organization's innovation support policies

There are many organizational factors that prevent workforces from effectively contributing toward advancing innovation in their organizations. Innovation ideation review meetings are, therefore, a huge opportunity for leaders and their followers to share some of the innovation barriers and how they can deal with them—also how they can make organization conditions more enabling for innovation and talk about innovation support strategies and policies that have produced results and why.

Example

Below is an example of an employee innovation ideation review table.

Table 4-4. Innovation- Ideation Review

Employee Innovation Ideation Review		
Name of employee(s): _____ Position: _____		
Department: _____		
Date: _____		
Period of time *(in terms of months)* being reviewed, from: _____ to: _____		
Innovation ideation goals set during the period under review: *What goals did the employee set?*	**Dimension of innovation:** If any innovation ideas were generated during the period under review, state the *type* and *degree* of each of the innovation ideas generated	**Development stage of the idea**: State whether the innovative idea generated has been subjected to the *innovation assessment and development process* of the organization. *If so, at what stage is the idea?*

table continues on next page

Innovation ideation goals set during the period under review: *What goals did the employee set?*	Dimension of innovation: If any innovation ideas were generated during the period under review, state the *type* and *degree* of each of the innovation ideas generated	Development stage of the idea: State whether the innovative idea generated has been subjected to the *innovation assessment and development process* of the organization. *If so, at what stage is the idea?*
Comments by supervisor or head of department	Comments by supervisor or head of department	Comments by supervisor and head of department
Employee's signature:		
Supervisor's signature:		
Head of department's signature:		

Step 13: Idea Assessment Progression Report

We mentioned in the introduction chapter that evaluating innovation performance of workforces contributes a great deal to the organization's mission of driving innovation across functional units and realizing innovation-led growth and competitiveness. The question is, how does the evaluation of workforce innovation contribute? As stated earlier, evaluating workforce innovation is embedded with tools and techniques that enhance the idea generation pipeline of the organization. An idea assessment progression report is yet another tool that can contribute a great deal to the innovation idea management process of an organization. Chapter Fourteen of the *Leadership for Innovation*, states that unless assessed and developed, innovation ideas are worthless and that the innovation idea management process plays this role. In this section we look at the idea assessment progression report in relation to the process of evaluating innovation performance of workforces.

This section covers: (1) the definition of an idea assessment progression report, (2) the importance of an idea assessment progression report, and (3) an example of a form for conducting the idea assessment progression report.

Definition

This book defines an idea assessment progression report as: *a regular report issued by the heads of departments and supervisors to employees that have submitted innovation ideas that states the status and progress of employees' innovative ideas that have been submitted to respective committees for further assessment and determination of innovative and investable potential.*

Importance

There are two reasons why it is important to conduct regular idea assessment progression reports:

Makes employees feel that their ideation efforts are appreciated
The idea assessment progression reports help to keep employees informed about what is happening with their ideas. By regularly informing employees

about the progress of their ideas, the employees will feel that their ideation efforts and contributions are being appreciated by the leadership. This encourages workforces to continue to generate ideas, even if some of their ideas do not make it for further development.

Helps workforces to understand the organization's innovation development system

One of the crucial elements for building an innovation-led growth and competitiveness is implementing an effective innovation development system embedded with tools for capturing, assessing, developing, and launching/ implementing innovation ideas into solutions that add commercial value to the organization. The idea assessment progress report affords leaders the ability to inform workforces about the various stages of assessment and development that innovative ideas are subjected to. This process exposes workforces to various aspects of the innovation development process, enabling employees to understand the organization's innovation development system which contributes to the aspect of winning the hearts and minds in contributing and championing innovation.

Example

Below is an example of a form (table 3-2) that can be used to determine the progress of innovation ideas undergoing assessment. The worksheet should be filled by a supervisor or head of department and should state the status of an employee's innovative idea undergoing assessment in the organization's innovation development process.

Table 4-5. Idea Assessment Progression Report

Name of department: _____	
Head of department: _____	
Date: _____	
Innovation idea assessment stages	**Comments on idea assessment status by the head of department**
1. Whether the innovation-idea has passed the initial idea screening stage	
2. Whether the innovation idea has passed the quick but detailed assessment stage	

table continues on next page

Innovation idea assessment stages	Comments on idea assessment status by the head of department
3. Whether the innovation idea has passed the stage for determining whether or not the idea has innovative and investible potential	
4. Whether the innovation idea has passed the project approval stage	
Comments by supervisor or head of department:	
Employee's name and signature:	
Both employee and the leader should retain a copy	

Chapter Fourteen of the *Leadership for Innovation* describe in detail an effective system for managing innovative ideas.

Step 14: Workforce Innovation Reward Model

We have, so far, looked at thirteen steps for designing and implementing a framework for evaluating workforce innovation across functional units. The last step is creating a model for rewarding workforces for their innovation performance.

From experience with organizational leaders, many companies have the desire to come up with a model for rewarding innovative thinking of their workforces, but the problem is that many companies lack the tools to do so. Remember, in the introduction chapter of this book, we cited a study by Institute for Corporate Productivity on the topic *Innovate or Perish: Building a Culture of Innovation*. The study revealed that one of the issues that executives are regularly wrestling with is how to reward employees for their innovative ideas. This section has suggested some approaches and tools for rewarding workforces for their innovation performance or innovative ideas.

This section covers: (1) the definition of the workforce innovation performance reward model, (2) the importance of the innovation reward model, (3) a checklist of aspects to consider when implementing the innovation performance reward system, and (4) an example of an innovation reward model.

Definition

A workforce innovation reward model is: *an integrated approach for determining how to reward workforces for their innovation performance or innovative ideas that have been developed and implemented /launched.*

Importance

The following are two reasons why an innovation performance reward policy is important.

It's a manifestation of the organization's commitment to workforce innovation

It is important for the leadership to bear in mind that employees have the inherent desire to contribute toward realizing the innovation potential of the company, and at the same time, they also want to maximize their individual benefits as they contribute toward innovation performance. This aspect must be exhibited not only in words, but in practice. One of the practical ways to show workforces how their involvement in innovation performance benefits their career development and economic well-being is by rewarding their inventiveness and innovativeness.

As explained in Chapter Eight of the *Leadership for Innovation*, rewarding workforces for innovation performance is vital because it's an effective way of winning the hearts and minds of workforces to own and contribute to the organization's culture of innovation. If workforces are not convinced there's something in it for them, they will likely exhibit unsupportive behavior toward championing innovation, such as:

- Being indifferent to all the innovation support initiatives that the company is implementing
- Withholding their innovative ideas
- Exploring other options to develop their ideas such as, licensing them
- Leaving the company and developing their innovative ideas elsewhere

Traditional performance appraisal rewards cannot drive workforce innovation

The introduction of this book observed that while many executives emphasize to workforces to regularly generate innovative ideas, organizational leaders still use traditional management models like performance appraisal rewards as a tool to encourage workforces to generate innovative ideas. As stated earlier, this book contests this practice because employees that are not well rewarded for innovation performance cannot meaningfully contribute to innovation.

There is an old performance cliché that says, *"What gets rewarded gets repeated!"* This phrase reminds me of B.F Skinner's (whose work I enjoyed during one of my post-grad courses) 'reward theory'. According to literature, Skinner, an American Psychologist, invented the operant conditioning chamber, also known as the *Skinner Box*. The box had a lever and a food tray. A hungry rat could get food delivered to the tray by pressing the lever. Skinner observed that when a rat was put in the box, it would wander around, sniffing and exploring, and would usually press the bar by accident, at which point a food pellet would drop into the tray. After that happened, the rate of bar pressing would increase dramatically and remain high until the rat was no longer hungry. Skinner was a firm believer of the idea that any human action was the result of the consequences of that same action. If the consequences were bad, there was a high chance that the action would not be repeated; however, if the consequences were good, the actions that lead to it would be reinforced. He called this the *principle of reinforcement.*

In the context of rewarding employees, it's pretty obvious that you can't get that which you are not rewarding employees for. In the terms of innovation performance, it means that if you reward workforces for innovation, you're likely to get innovation-related or aligned behavior! On the other hand, you'll get zero innovation-related behavior if you don't reward workforces for it! For this reason, it's vital to enact innovation aligned reward practices if the organization leadership wants a reward to play a role in advancing workforce innovation across functional units.

Checklist of Aspects to Consider

Here is checklist of some of the important aspects to take into consideration when implementing the innovation performance reward system. This enhances the effectiveness of the tool.

- Conduct a simple situation analysis to determine whether innovation has been aligned to the company's compensation or reward system. If yes, is there room for improvement?
- Form a committee to come up with proposals of innovation performance reward models.
- Once an innovation performance reward model is designed, the leadership should form a committee responsible for promoting the

innovation performance reward model across the organization and educate staff about it.

- Once implemented the leadership should periodically evaluate and make improvements to the innovation performance reward model, where necessary.

Example of an Innovation Reward Model

Here is an example of an innovation performance reward model. The model is structured in three parts:

- Part A: Description of the Innovation Idea
- Part B: Business Result Contribution
- Part C: Innovation Cash Reward Model

We return to our fictitious company Walu Insurance. Assuming Walu Insurance is implementing an innovation performance reward model for its business units and functional units.

Core units
- Home insurance
- Auto insurance
- Business insurance
- Life insurance
- Health insurance
- Marketing
- Customer service

Support Units
- HR
- IT
- Procurement
- Finance and accounting

Table 4-6. Workforce Innovation Reward Model

Part A
Description of the Innovation Idea

1. Name of innovation or innovation idea under consideration:

   _____

   _____

2. Name of employee(s) behind the innovation:

   _____

   _____

3. State the type of innovation (Is it a product innovation, service innovation, process innovation, marketing innovation or customer service innovation?):

   _____

   _____

4. State the innovation degree (Is it a radical or incremental innovation?):

   _____

   _____

5. **Value:** Outline the value or solution that the innovation under consideration has created:

   _____

   _____

6. **Problem solved**: Outline the problem/ need that the innovation under consideration has fixed:

   _____

   _____

7. **Business opportunity:** Outline the opportunity that the innovation under consideration has created, captured, or discovered for the company:

   _____

   _____

Part B

Categories of Financial Result Contribution

This part outlines two contexts of financial contributions from innovations under consideration: revenue generation innovations - (**Section I**) and cost savings innovations - (**Section II**). We've also included **Section III** for customer service innovations whose financial contribution in most cases are difficult to measure or determine.

Section I: Revenue Generation Innovations

Revenue generation innovations are the kind of innovations whose financial contribution is in the form of revenue.

So, questions in this section should be phrased in the context of revenue generation from particular types of innovation such as: product innovations, service innovations, market innovations such as, , pricing innovation, promotion innovation, or new markets that have been discovered for existing insurance products or services.

Questions:

- How much revenue did the innovation under consideration contribute during the period under review?

  _____

  _____

  _____

- Are you able to project how much revenue the innovation will contribute to the company over the next two to three years? If yes, indicate the projection:

  _____

  _____

  _____

table continues on next page

Section II: Cost Saving Innovations

Cost saving innovations are innovations whose financial contribution is in the form of cost saving.

In most cases, these innovations fall under process innovations and innovations in support functional units. For Walu Insurance, process innovations would be implemented in all the five business units (home insurance, auto insurance, business insurance, life insurance, health insurance) and core functional units such as, marketing department, customer service department. Cost saving innovations would also be implemented in the support functional unit: HR, IT, procurement, finance and accounting.

To determine cost saving innovation, questions should be phrased in the context of innovations aimed at cutting costs.

Questions:

- How much money has the company saved over the period under review as a result of the cost saving innovation under consideration?

  _____

  _____

  _____

- How much money is the company expected to save over the next two to three years as a result of the cost saving innovation under consideration?

  _____

  _____

  _____

table continues on next page

Section III: Customer Service Innovations

In most cases, as mentioned earlier, it's difficult to quantify how much revenue has been generated as a result of a customer service innovation. So, the leadership should come up with a separate model for rewarding customer service innovations. Some of the factors that could be taken into consideration when determining the efficacy of a particular customer service innovation (i.e. before-purchase customer service, during purchase customer service or after service innovation) in relation to its contribution towards financial results could include:

- Is there clear evidence that the customer service innovation under consideration has attracted or retained a significant number of customers?
- In management's view, has the customer service innovation under consideration improved or enhanced the customer service reputation of the company to the outside world?
- Has the customer service innovation under consideration been voted as one of the best, for example, five or so customer service innovations by staff during the period under review?

Part C

Innovation Cash Reward Model

(This model is divided into three sections; I, II & III)

This model has suggested three perspectives of determining workforce innovation cash rewards; namely:

- Revenue generation innovations (Section I)
- Cost reduction innovations (Section II)
- Cash reward worksheet for customer service innovations (Section III)

Section I: Revenue Generation Innovations

As indicated in Part B, innovations add commercial value to companies in different contexts. Therefore, innovation performance rewards should be based on how the innovation contributes to the financial results of the company. That is, whether or not the financial contribution of a particular innovation is in the form of revenue or cost reduction.

table continues on next page

The following is an example of how to determine workforce innovation cash rewards for:

- Revenue generation innovations
- Cost reduction innovations

Cash Rewards for Revenue Generation Innovations

(We suggested two stages for this category)

Stages:

1. First stage involves creating a worksheet for determining revenue generated by a particular innovation over a given period:

Assuming a particular type of innovation launched by Walu Insurance's home insurance business unit is projected to generate some revenue over a period of five years, as indicated below:

2019	2020	2021	2022	2023
$1m - $3m	$4m - $5m	$6m - $10m	$11m - $15m	$16m-$20m

Question:

In such a scenario, the leadership should have a framework in place stating how much cash rewards would be offered to an employee if their innovation generated the above revenues over a period of five years.

2. Second stage involves creating cash reward options. An example of the two options are :

- To create a table of predetermined cash rewards that would be offered for each range of revenues generated by the innovation under consideration.
- To offer employees cash rewards equivalent to: 2, 3, 4, or 5 times their current monthly or annual salary for each range of revenues generated over a period of time.

table continues on next page

Section II: Cost Saving Innovations

As indicated in Section B, cost saving innovations are innovations whose financial contribution is in form of cost savings made by the company as a result of a particular cost saving innovation under consideration.

Note: All categories of cost saving innovations should be outlined clearly in the organization's manual for evaluating workforce innovation.

Cash Rewards for Cost Saving Innovations

(There are two stages for this category)

Stages:

1. First stage involves creating a worksheet for determining the cost savings of a particular innovation over a given period:

Assuming Walu Insurance has launched a particular type of cost saving innovation which is projected to make the following savings for the company over a period of five years, as indicated below:

2019	2020	2021	2022	2023
$1m - $1.5m	$1.5m - $2m	$2m - $3.5m	$3.5m - $4m	$4m-$5m

Note:

The company should have a framework outlining cash rewards that would be offered to an employee whose innovation is projected to benefit the company in terms of cost savings, as indicated above, over a period of five years.

2. Second stage involves designing cash reward options. An example of the two options are:
   - Create a table of predetermined cash rewards that would be offered for each range of cost savings made by an innovation.
   - Offer employees cash rewards equivalent to: 2, 3, 4, or 5 times their current monthly or annual salary for each range of revenues generated over a period of time.

table continues on next page

Section III: Cash reward for innovations whose financial contribution is difficult to determine, e.g. customer service innovations

Remember, in Part B of this framework we mentioned that is it's difficult to quantify financial results or contributions by some innovations.

In this section we've suggested a simple innovation quotient procedure that can be applied to determine cash rewards in scenarios where it's difficult to determine the financial contribution or amount of revenue generated by an innovation. There are about five stages in this procedure.

1. Determining whether the innovation is incremental or radical, awarding points appropriately, for example:

    -   Incremental innovation =**10 points** (these are guaranteed points, i.e. bonus points for having made it to that stage of the innovation development process).
    -   Radical innovation = **20 points** (these are guaranteed points, i.e. bonus points for having made it to that stage of the innovation development process).

2. Identifying a set of factors that will be applied as a guide to determine the nature and significance of the value the innovation makes the activities of the functional unit. For instance, let's assume we're determining a customer service innovation. The following are some of the factors that could be considered:

    -   The extent to which the customer service innovation contributed toward improving or enhancing the company's image
    -   The extent to which the customer service innovation contributed to attracting and retaining customers
    -   The extent to which the customer service innovation contributed to sorting out some customer complaints

table continues on next page

71

3. Creating a structure for predetermined set of points, which are outlined in a table against selected factors/aspects of significance in the context of a particular type of innovation. The predetermined set of points will be allocated based on the strength of the contribution that, for example, the *customer service innovation* makes in relation to the factor or aspect under consideration. An example of a set of four points would be: **20-25-30-35.** You only allocate or reward one number per factor. So, assuming we were considering customer service innovation "**X**". For illustration's sake, let's say the perception is that customer service innovation "**X**" has contributed to------"*improving the company's image*" and the points will be allocated or rewarded based on one's judgement of how much the customer service innovation "**X**" has contributed to the aspect of "*improving the company's image*", we could allocate or award **30 points**.

Below is an example of a simple table outlining factors for determining the significance of the contribution made by a customer service innovation under consideration and point options to be allocated to each significance of contribution by the innovation under consideration:

Factors for determining the significance of contribution made by the customer service innovation	Point options to be allocated to each significance of contribution by the innovation under consideration
Contributed toward improving or enhancing the company's image	**20-25-30-35** (you could allocate 35)
Contributed to attracting and retaining customers	**40-45-50-55** (you could allocate 45 points)
Contributed to sorting out some customer complaints	**55-60-65-70** (you could allocate 65 points)
Then add all points awarded	**145**

table continues on next page

4. Adding all the points allocated, then determining the significance level of the contribution of the customer service innovation under consideration by using a predetermined range of ratings, such as shown below:

Significance level of contribution	Corresponding range of ratings for each level of significance
Low significance	0-55
Average significance	55-110
Moderate significance	110-145
High significance	145-160
Exceptional significance	160-180

5. Applying the *significance level* of contribution that has been calculated to determine *cash rewards* that employees will be entitled to for their innovation. In the table below we have suggested a number of mechanisms for determining the amount of cash rewards.

Low significance	Average significance	Moderate significance	High significance	Exceptional significance
$1,000	$2,000	$3,000	$5,000	$10,000
Equivalent of employee's monthly salary	Equivalent of 2x the employee's monthly salary	Equivalent of 3x the employee's monthly salary	Equivalent of 4x the employee's monthly salary	Equivalent of 5x the employee's monthly salary
5% of the employee's annual salary	10% of the employee's annual salary	15% of the employee's annual salary	30% of the employee's annual salary	70% of the employee's annual salary

Note: You should include a statement outlining how the payments will be structured, i.e. if it be quarterly, twice a year, or annually.

Workforce Innovation Recognition Award Programs

In addition to rewarding staff with cash and other incentives for innovation performance, you could also come up with tailor-made workforce innovation recognition awards.

Many studies and authorities on employee recognition have revealed that recognition awards have an impact on employee retention and commitment. Since this section is not aimed at exploring recognition awards, we suggest that you take a look at a number of surveys conducted by human resources organizations on the topic of employee recognition. One such organization is WorldatWork. You could also check work done by Dr. Bob Nelson, an authority on employee recognition.

Here are some aspects that the leadership should consider when creating and managing a workforce innovation recognition award program:

- Create a committee that will be mandated to come up with a proposal for the workforce innovation recognition award model.
- Once created, the committee should come up with an action plan for designing and managing the workforce innovation recognition award model. See a sample of an action plan for managing recognition award program below:

Table 4-7. Example of Action Plan for Recognition Award

Objective: To create an action plan of programs and strategies for managing a workforce innovation recognition award program				
Activities: List of activities and events that HR will conduct to contribute toward developing and implementing the workforce innovation recognition award program---(here are some examples of activities)	**Time-frame:** the actionable timeframe within which each listed task shall be completed	**Who:** Individuals or subcommittee who is responsible for undertaking the task	**Resources:** The resources needed to undertake each task	**Outcome:** Completed deliverables in terms of--- implementation of various activities for managing the workforce innovation recognition program
Activities **Such as:** 1. Conduct a situational analysis to determine the kind of innovation award recognition programs the company has and identify aspects that need improvement.				

table continues on next page

2. Come up with different categories and levels of recognition award models for innovations generated by staff. For instance, • Platinum Recognition Award for Innovation Performance • Gold Recognition Award for Innovation Performance • Diamond Recognition Award for Innovation Performance **Note:** The recognition criteria should clearly spell out the level of innovation contribution to achieve a designated recognition, i.e. number of patents, number of innovations, amount of revenue generated, or cost savings that an innovation should contribute to qualify for a particular level of recognition.			

table continues on next page

Other recognition awards could include: *"Certificate of Recognition"* which could be given to employees for their contribution toward building the culture of innovation in the company, such as: 1. Constant generation of innovative ideas, even though none of them have been implemented as innovations. • Generation of ideas that contribute to advancing and sustaining innovation performance across the organization.				
Evaluation: Identify the dates for conducting evaluations to determine how this action plan is progressing				
Date:	**Date:**	**Date:**	**Date:**	**Date:**
State aspects that will be evaluated on this date	State aspects that will be evaluated on this date	State aspects that will be evaluated on this date	State aspects that will be evaluated on this date	State aspects that will be evaluated on this date

Action Plan for Creating and Implementing Mechanism for Evaluating Workforce Innovation Performance

We end the book with an example of a simple action plan for creating a program for evaluating workforce innovation performance. Here is an example of a table for creating an action plan:

Table 4-8. Action Plan for Evaluating Workforce Innovation Performance

Walu Insurance				
Name of committee:				
Name and positions of committee members:				
Date:				
Timeline:				
Objective: To create an action plan for designing and implementing a mechanism for evaluating workforce innovation performance				
Activities: List of tasks to be undertaken to contribute toward implementing a framework for evaluating innovation performance of workforces (see examples of tasks below)	**Timeframe:** Actionable time-frame within which each listed task shall be completed	**Who:** Individuals or subcommittee that is responsible for undertaking the tasks	**Resources:** Resources needed to undertake each task	**Outcome:** Completed booklet outlining steps for evaluating innovation performance of workforces

table continues on next page

Task: To conduct a situation analysis for determining whether workforce innovation performance is included in the organization's current performance appraisal practices **<u>Activities</u>** **1.** **2.** **3.** **4.**				

table continues on next page

Task: To outline the organizational vision, i.e. what the organization would prefer to be like after a specific period **Activities** 1. 2. 3. 4. 5.				
Task: To educate workforces about the importance of evaluating innovation performance in realizing the organization vision **Activities** 1. 2. 3. 4.				

table continues on next page

Task: Outline *core* and *support* functional units **<u>Activities</u>** 1. 2. 3. 4.				
Task: Educating workforces about the meaning of innovation **<u>Activities</u>** 1. 2. 3. 4.				
Task: Educate workforces on dimensions of innovation **<u>Activities</u>** 1. 2. 3. 4.				

table continues on next page

Task: Align the meaning of innovation to functional units and business segments **<u>Activities</u>** **1.** **2.** **3.** **4.**				
Task: To integrate innovation performance roles in job positions **<u>Activities</u>** **1.** **2.** **3.** **4.**				

table continues on next page

Task: To educate workforces about factors driving innovation in functional units **<u>Activities</u>** 1. 2. 3. 4.			
Task: To create innovation goals **<u>Activities</u>** 1. 2. 3. 4.			

table continues on next page

Task: To educate workforces on how to create innovation ideation goals **Activities** 1. 2. 3. 4.				
Task: Complete the innovation idea submission procedure **Activities** 1. 2. 3. 4.				

table continues on next page

Task: To create an employee innovation ideation review process **<u>Activities</u>** 1. 2. 3. 4.				
Task: To create an innovation idea assessment progression process **<u>Activities</u>** 1. 2. 3. 4.				

table continues on next page

Task: To create an innovation performance reward model **<u>Activities</u>** **1.** **2.** **3.** **4.** **5.**				
Evaluation: Identify the dates for conducting evaluations to determine how this action plan is progressing				
Date:	**Date:**	**Date:**	**Date:**	**Date:**
Outline aspects that will be evaluated on this date	Outline aspects that will be evaluated on this date	Outline aspects that will be evaluated on this date	Outline aspects that will be evaluated on this date	Outline aspects that will be evaluated on this date

SUMMARY

Let's recap the six main aspects this book has covered:

1. Studies have revealed that one of the issues that executives are constantly wrestling with is how to evaluate the innovation performance of employees and how to reward employees for their innovation performance.
2. Workforce innovation performance is defined as a process that involves collecting, analyzing, and recording data about innovation abilities and the innovation performance of individual employees.
3. The three types of innovation performance roles are: innovative thinking duties, innovation engagement duties, and innovation management duties.
4. The objectives of evaluating workforce innovation performance are described.
5. Out of the three types of innovation performance roles, this book focuses on how to evaluate and reward the innovative thinking-related performance of workforces.
6. This book is segmented into Four Chapters and structured into Fourteen Steps, designing and implementing a mechanism for evaluating workforce innovation.

SELECTED REFERENCES

https://www.hrbartender.com/images/Capitalizing_on_Complexity.pdf

https://www.conference-board.org/ceo-challenge2015/

https://www.businessnewsdaily.com

https://www.i4cp.com/productivity-blog/2011/07/12/want-more-innovation-hire-for-it

https://www.quora.com/What-is-B-F-Skinners-theory-of-behavior

David Masumba, *Leadership for Innovation*, New York, Morgan James Publishing, 2019

www.ingramcontent.com/pod-product-compliance
Lightning Source LLC
Chambersburg PA
CBHW021950190326
41519CB00009B/1209